AF867531

MathFlare

Name: ______________________

Class: __________

Teacher: ______________________

Copyright © 2024 MathFlare Publishing.
All rights reserved. This book or any portion thereof may not be reproduced or used in any manner whatsoever without the express written permission of the publisher except for the use of brief quotations in a book review.

Introduction

As parents and educators, we recognize the pivotal role mathematics plays in shaping a child's academic journey and future success. Yet, the path to mathematical proficiency can often seem daunting, fraught with challenges and complexities. That's where the transformative power of MathFlare Workbooks shine through, illuminating the way forward with clarity, precision, and purpose.

Introducing MathFlare Workbooks – a beacon of guidance, a testament to excellence, and a catalyst for achievement. Crafted with meticulous care and expertise, MathFlare Workbooks stand as paragons of educational excellence, designed to nurture young minds, ignite a passion for learning, and develop a deep-rooted understanding of mathematical concepts.

Picture this: your child eagerly delves into the pages of Mathflare Workbook, greeted by a step-by-step guide illuminated with vivid examples that demystify complex mathematical concepts. With each turn of the page, they embark on a journey of discovery, encountering thoughtfully curated practice questions that reinforce learning and hone problem-solving skills. And when they unveil the answers to those very questions, a sense of accomplishment blossoms within them – a tangible reward for their hard work and dedication.

But MathFlare Workbooks are more than just tools for learning; they are pathways to comprehension, fostering a deep-seated understanding of mathematical concepts through a sequential, logical flow. From fundamental principles to advanced problem-solving strategies, every chapter builds upon the last, ensuring a robust foundation upon which future knowledge can be constructed.

As parents, we yearn for nothing more than to see our children thrive, to witness the spark of inspiration ignited within them as they conquer academic challenges with confidence and poise. MathFlare Workbooks serve as partners in this noble endeavor, offering not just practice questions, but the keys to unlocking a world of opportunity.

And for teachers, MathFlare Workbooks stand as invaluable allies in the quest to cultivate mathematical proficiency in the classroom. With answers readily available, instructors can focus on guiding and nurturing their students, confident in the knowledge that MathFlare Workbooks provide a solid framework upon which to build.

In the pages of MathFlare Workbooks, we find not just the promise of academic excellence, but the seeds of a brighter tomorrow. So let us embrace the power of mathematics, let us champion the journey of learning, and let us pave the way for a generation of young minds poised to shape the world. With MathFlare Workbooks as our guide, the possibilities are infinite, and the future, bright.

Table of Contents

MathFlare
2
MATH WORKBOOK
Step by Step Guide and Essential Practice with Answers
Addition Subtraction
Multiplication
Place Value and Expanded Notations
Geometry
MathFlare Publishing

MathFlare
2-3
MATH WORKBOOK
Step by Step Guide and Essential Practice with Answers
Addition Subtraction
Multiplication and Division
Place Value and Expanded Notations
Geometry
MathFlare Publishing

MathFlare
3
MATH WORKBOOK
Step by Step Guide and Essential Practice with Answers
Multiplication and Division
Decimals
Place Value and Expanded Notations
Fractions and Geometry
MathFlare Publishing

MathFlare
1
MATH WORKBOOK
Step by Step Guide and Essential Practice with Answers
Counting and Numbers
Addition and Subtraction
Place Value and Expanded Notations
Understanding Time
MathFlare Publishing

MathFlare
1-2
MATH WORKBOOK
Step by Step Guide and Essential Practice with Answers
Counting and Numbers
Addition and Subtraction
Place Value and Expanded Notations
Understanding Time
MathFlare Publishing

MathFlare
3-4
MATH WORKBOOK
Step by Step Guide and Essential Practice with Answers
Addition Subtraction
Multiplication Division
Place Value and Expanded Notations
Fractions and Geometry
MathFlare Publishing

MathFlare
4
MATH WORKBOOK
Step by Step Guide and Essential Practice with Answers
Addition Subtraction
Multiplication Division
Place Value and Expanded Notations
Fractions and Geometry
MathFlare Publishing

MathFlare
4-5
MATH WORKBOOK
Step by Step Guide and Essential Practice with Answers
Multiplication Division
Place Value and Expanded Notations
Fractions and Geometry
Unit Conversion
MathFlare Publishing

MathFlare
5
MATH
WORKBOOK
Step by Step Guide and Essential Practice with Answers
Multiplication Division
Place Value and Expanded Notations
Fractions and Geometry
Unit Conversion
MathFlare Publishing

MathFlare
5-6
MATH
WORKBOOK
Step by Step Guide and Essential Practice with Answers
Multiplication Division
Place Value and Expanded Notations
Fractions and Geometry
Units and Statistics
MathFlare Publishing

MathFlare
6
MATH
WORKBOOK
Step by Step Guide and Essential Practice with Answers
Integers and Statistics
Arithmetic and Pre-Algebra
Fractions and Geometry
Ratio and Percentage
MathFlare Publishing

MathFlare
6-7
MATH
WORKBOOK
Step by Step Guide and Essential Practice with Answers
Arithmetic and Pre-Algebra
Ratio, Percent Proportion
Geometry
Statistics
MathFlare Publishing

MathFlare
7
MATH
WORKBOOK
Step by Step Guide and Essential Practice with Answers
Pre-Algebra
Ratio, Percent Proportion
Geometry
Statistics
MathFlare Publishing

MathFlare
7-8
MATH
WORKBOOK
Step by Step Guide and Essential Practice with Answers
Pre-Algebra
Ratio, Percent Proportion
Geometry and Cartesian Plane
Statistics
MathFlare Publishing

MathFlare
8-9
MATH
WORKBOOK
Step by Step Guide and Essential Practice with Answers
Pre-Algebra
Ratio, Proportion and Percentage
Linear Equations
Geometry and Cartesian Plane
MathFlare Publishing

MathFlare
8
MATH
WORKBOOK
Step by Step Guide and Essential Practice with Answers
Pre-Algebra
Percentage
Linear Equations
Geometry
MathFlare Publishing

Order of Operations (PEMDAS)

The order of operations, often remembered by the acronym PEMDAS, stands for:

- **Parentheses**: Perform operations inside parentheses first.
- **Exponents**: Evaluate exponents (powers and roots) next.
- **Multiplication and Division**: Perform multiplication and division from left to right.
- **Addition and Subtraction:** Perform addition and subtraction from left to right.

The order of operations helps to clarify which operations should be performed first in a mathematical expression to ensure consistent and accurate results.

- **Parentheses**: Evaluate expressions within parentheses first. If there are nested parentheses, start with the innermost ones and work your way out.
    1. Example: $2 \times (3 + 4) = 2 \times 7 = 14$
- **Exponents**: Evaluate expressions with exponents (powers and roots) next.
    1. Example: $2^3 + 4 = 8 + 4 = 12$
- **Multiplication and Division**: Perform multiplication and division from left to right.
    1. Example: $2 \times 3 + 4 = 6 + 4 = 10$
    2. Example: $6 \div 2 \times 3 = 3 \times 3 = 9$
- **Addition and Subtraction**: Perform addition and subtraction from left to right.
    1. Example: $2 + 3 \times 4 = 2 + 12 = 14$
    2. Example: $10 - 4 \div 2 = 10 - 2 = 8$

Solving Equations (One Side)

Solving one-step equations involves performing a single operation to isolate the variable and find its value.

Let's solve an equation step by step: $16 + x = 31$

1. **Identify the Goal:**

   The goal is to isolate the variable x on one side of the equation.

2. **Simplify the Equation:** Combine like terms on both sides of the equation, if necessary.

   The equation is already simplified.

3. **Undo Addition or Subtraction:** If there's addition or subtraction involving the variable, undo it by performing the opposite operation on both sides of the equation.

   Since x is being added to 16, we'll undo this operation by subtracting 16 from both sides of the equation:

   $$16 + x - 16 = 31 - 16$$

4. **Isolate the Variable:** Ensure that the variable is alone on one side of the equation.

   $$X = 15$$

5. **Check Your Solution:** Substitute the value of x back into the original equation to verify that it satisfies the equation.

   $$16 + 15 = 31$$

   $$31 = 31$$

   The equation is balanced, so the solution.

Equations (Two Sides)

A two-sided equation is an equation where both sides have expressions with variables and constants. The goal when solving a two-sided equation is to find the value of the variable that makes both sides equal.

For example: Let's solve an equation:

$$9 + 8x + 8 = 64 + x + 2$$

- **Combine Like Terms:** Simplify each side of the equation by combining like terms (terms with the same variable or constants).

$$9 + 8x + 8 = 64 + x + 2$$

$$17 + 8x = 66 + x$$

- **Isolate the Variable:** Use inverse operations to isolate the variable on one side of the equation.

subtract x from both sides:

$$17 + 8x - x = 66 + x - x$$

$$17 + 7x = 66$$

subtracting 17 from both sides:

$$17 - 17 + 7x = 66 - 17$$

$$7x = 49$$

divide both sides by 7:

$$\frac{7x}{7} = \frac{49}{7} = x = 7$$

- **Check Solution:** Once you find the solution, substitute it back into the original equation to ensure it makes t ation true.

Substitute $x = 7$ back into the original equation:

$$9 + 8(7) + 8 = 64 + 7 + 2$$

$$9 + 56 + 8 = 64 + 7 + 24$$

$$73 = 73$$

Solving Inequalities

Inequalities are mathematical expressions that compare the relative sizes of two values. They are used to express relationships where one quantity is:

- "<" (less than),
- ">" (greater than),
- "<=" (less than or equal to),
- ">=" (greater than or equal to),
- and "≠" (not equal to) another quantity.

For example:

$$y + -10 \leq -8$$

To isolate y, we need to get rid of the constant term –10. Since –10 is being subtracted from y, we can undo this operation by adding 10 to both sides of the inequality:

$$y - 10 + 10 \leq -8 + 10$$

$$y \leq 2$$

To check the solution:

$$2 - 10 \leq -8$$

$$-8 = -8$$

The inequality is true when $y = 2$

Name:______________ Date: ___________

Order of Operations (PEMDAS)

Evaluate Expressions.

1. $3 + 4 + 2 =$

2. $(4^2) \times (2^2) + 9 =$

3. $(8 + 3) \div 8 =$

4. $9 + 9 - 3 + 7 =$

5. $(6^2) \times (9^2) + 2 =$

6. $6 + 1^2 + 5 + 5^2 =$

7. $7(8 + 7) =$

8. $(5 \times 9) - (6 + 7) =$

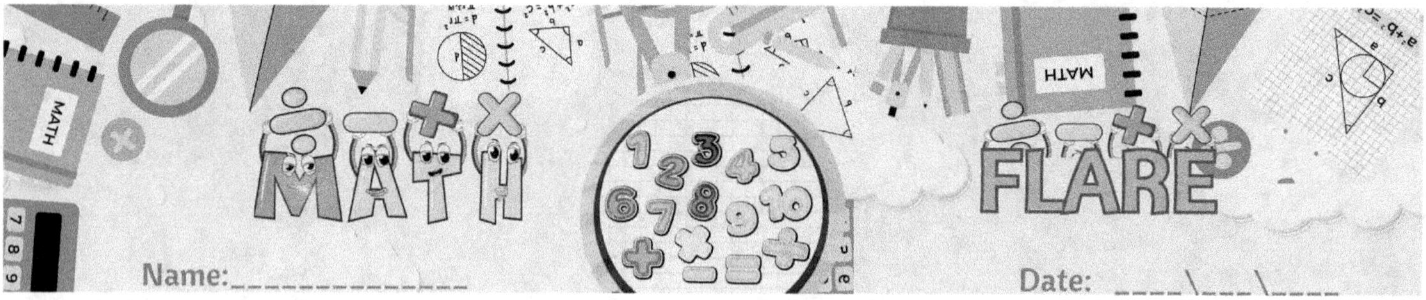

Name:______________ Date: ____________

9. $2 + 3^2 =$

10. $9(3 + 6) =$

11. $(2 + 1)^2 =$

12. $2 + 9^2 + 7 + 6^2 =$

13. $1 \times 2 + 3 =$

14. $(2^2) \times (7^2) + 2 =$

15. $4 + 7 + 9 =$

16. $(5 + 9) \times (3 + 9) =$

17. $7 \times 9 =$

18. $3(1 + 5) =$

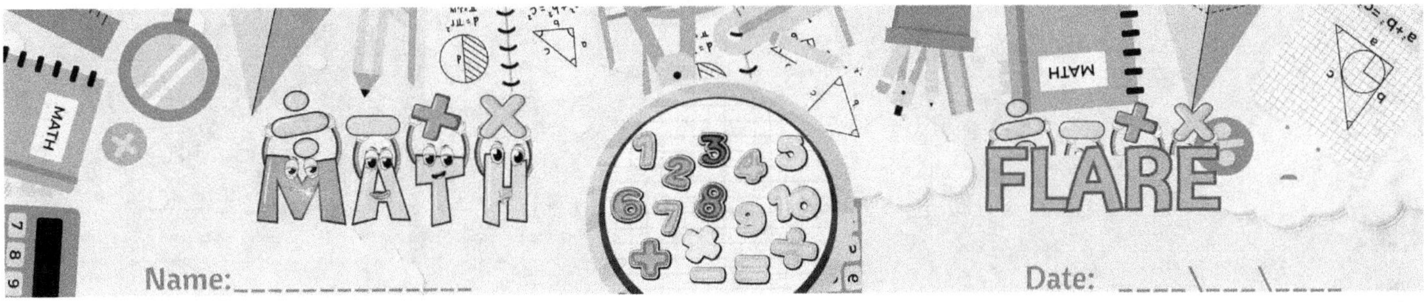

19. $(7 + 8)^2 + (5 + 6)^2 =$

20. $(2 \times 7) - (1 + 9) =$

21. $(7^2) \times (4^2) + 2 =$

22. $7 \times (5 + 10) =$

23. $(5 + 10)^2 + (1 + 4)^2 =$

24. $(3 + 5)^2 =$

25. $(2 + 5) \times (2 + 2) =$

26. $(8 + 3)^2 + (3 + 1)^2 =$

27. $(1 + 6)^2 + (7 + 10)^2 =$

28. $10 + 8 + 3 =$

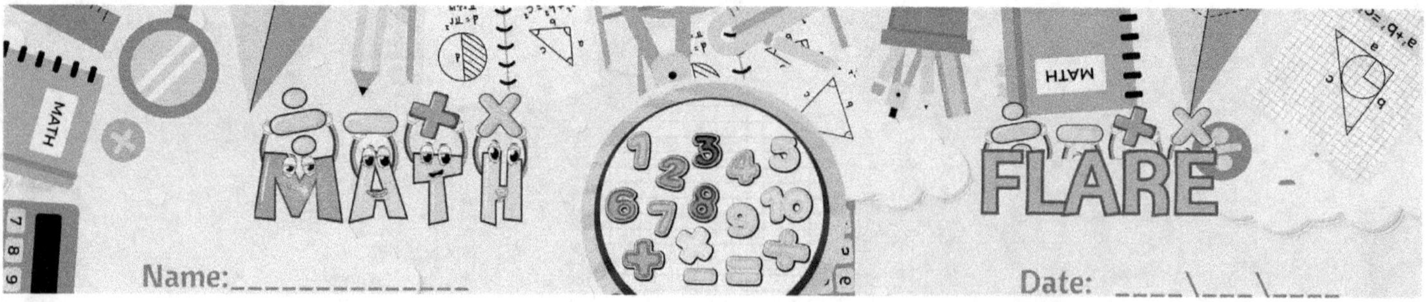

29. $(10^2) \times (2^2) + 5 =$

30. $(10^2) \times (6^2) + 2 =$

31. $(8 + 6)(10 + 6) =$

32. $3 + 10^2 =$

33. $(10 + 8)(9 + 7) =$

34. $5 \times (10 + 6) =$

35. $4 + 2 + 6 =$

36. $3 \times 9 \times 10 =$

37. $(4 + 10)^2 =$

38. $9 \times (1 + 7) =$

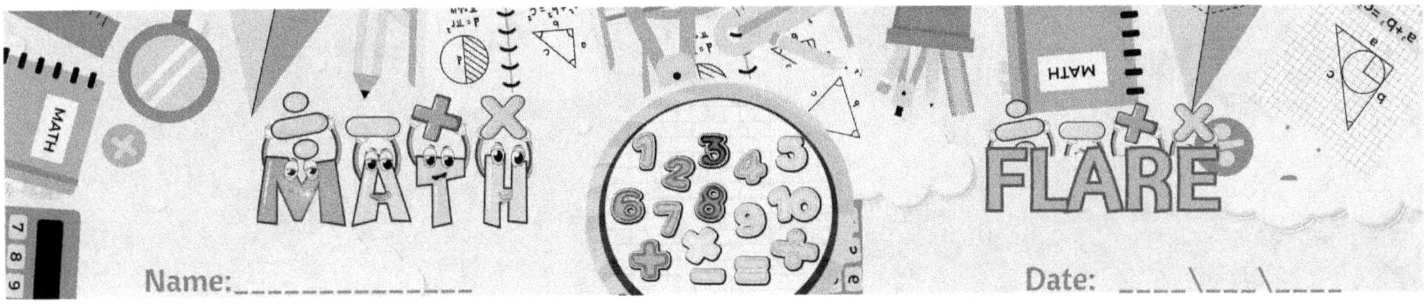

39. $(3 \times 7) - (8 + 8) =$

40. $(6 \times 9) - (6 + 4) =$

41. $(7 + 4) \div 4 =$

42. $10 + 2^2 + 7 + 5^2 =$

43. $3 \times 4 + 3 =$

44. $2 + 10 - 3 + 10 =$

45. $4 + 4 + 1 + 4 =$

46. $9 \times (7 + 1) =$

47. $3 + 2 + 10 + 6 =$

48. $(3 \times 4) - (6 + 3) =$

49. $2 \times 3 \times 1 =$

50. $(1 + 2) \times (3 + 3) =$

51. $1 + 3^2 =$

52. $(4 + 7)^2 =$

53. $(4 + 7)^2 + (1 + 8)^2 =$

54. $(7 + 1)(5 + 3) =$

55. $3 \times 4 \times 8 =$

56. $(3^2) \times (10^2) + 9 =$

57. $4 + 5 - 3 + 4 =$

58. $(4^2) \times (10^2) + 3 =$

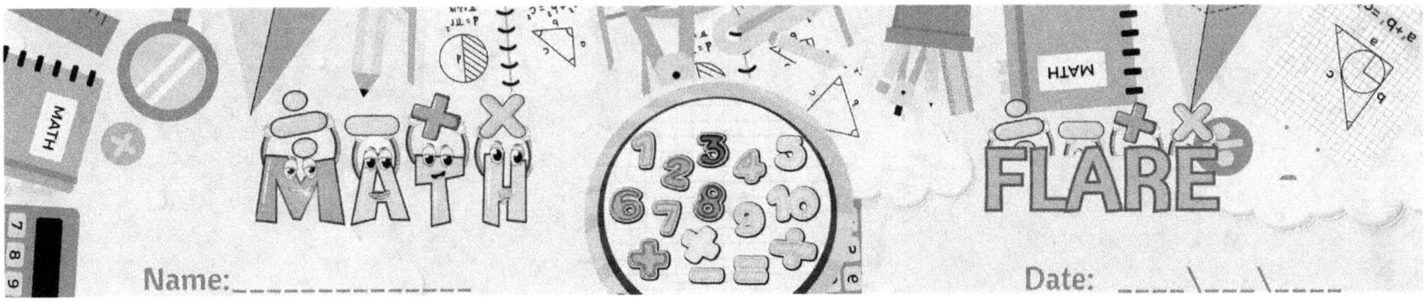

59. $(9^2) \times (10^2) + 2 =$

60. $10 + 2 + 10 + 2 =$

61. $(8 + 2)(4 + 8) =$

62. $(10^2) \times (3^2) + 4 =$

63. $4 + 2^2 =$

64. $(4 + 3)^2 + (6 + 9)^2 =$

65. $2 + 4 + 10 =$

66. $5 + 1 + 1 =$

67. $2 \times 8 \times 8 =$

68. $(10 + 7)(9 + 5) =$

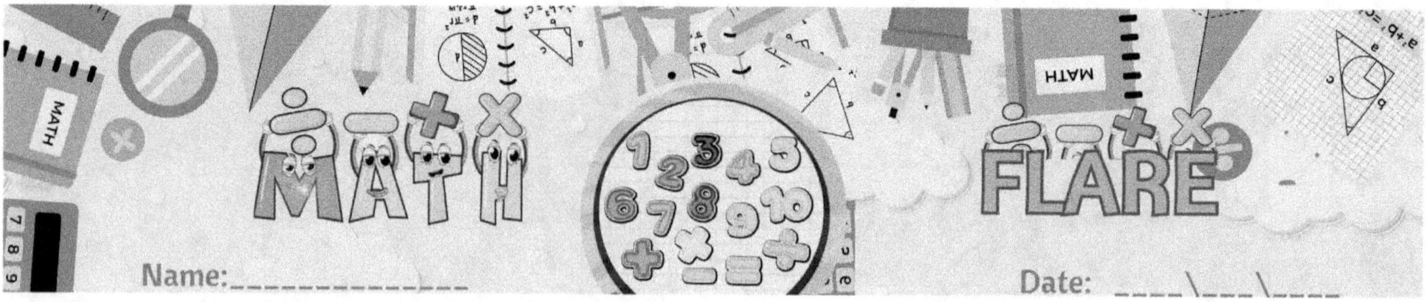

Equations (One Side)

Solve for the variable.

69. $5 \times k = 40$

70. $4z - 5 = 3$

71. $2 \times y = 20$

72. $y \div 8 = 6$

73. $9 \div k = 9$

74. $2 + k = 8$

75. $10 + 8k = 26$

76. $9 - y = 4$

77. $9k + 3 = 66$

78. $5 \times k = 35$

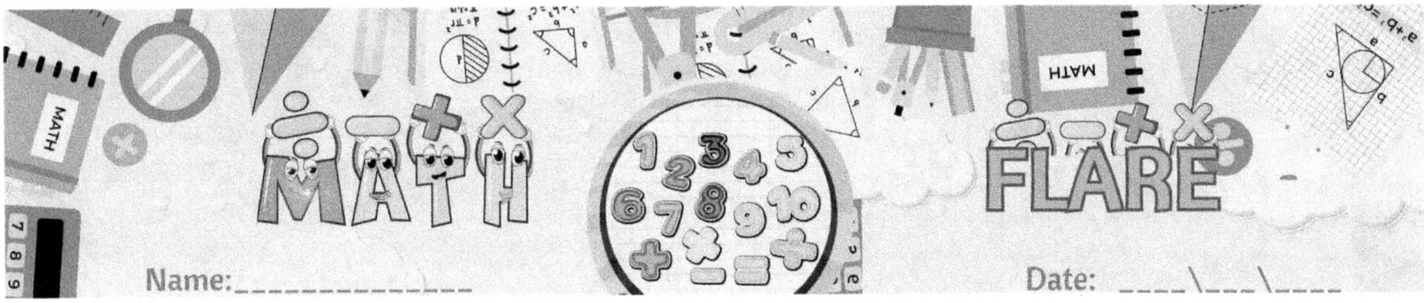

79. $k + 6 = 14$

80. $2y + 8 = 18$

81. $3z + 1 = 13$

82. $k - 4 = 3$

83. $k \div 4 = 10$

84. $2 - z = 1$

85. $6 - x = 2$

86. $y \div 3 = 5$

87. $z \div 9 = 2$

88. $1 \times m = 2$

89. $6 + z = 8$

90. $k - 6 = 3$

Name:______________

Date: ___________

91. $m \times 2 = 6$

92. $1z + 10 = 14$

93. $m \times 5 = 50$

94. $5x + 8 = 48$

95. $33 - 5z = 3$

96. $y + 4 = 5$

97. $8 - y = 6$

98. $k \times 5 = 15$

99. $14 - 4z = 6$

100. $1 + z = 7$

101. $9 + x = 12$

102. $27 - 6k = 9$

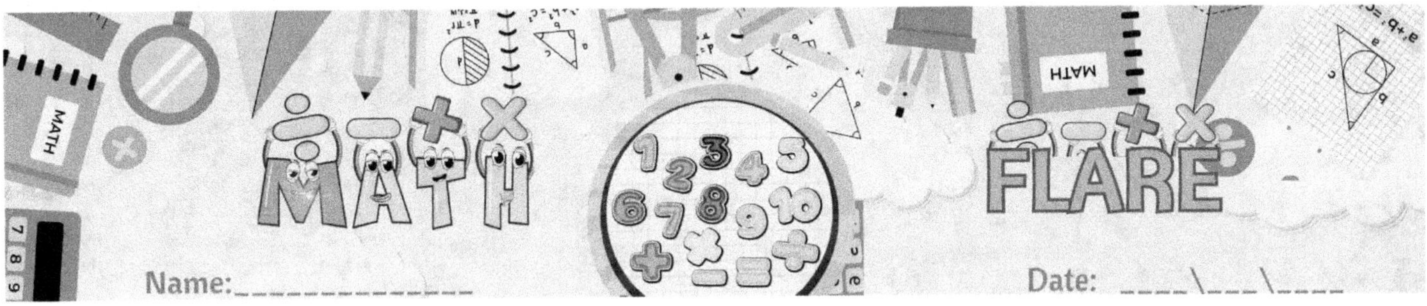

103. $m \div 1 = 10$

104. $4 + k = 13$

105. $k \div 6 = 6$

106. $5 + 7x = 40$

107. $z + 1 = 10$

108. $6 - x = 2$

109. $14 \div k = 7$

110. $3 + 6y = 57$

111. $8 \div k = 1$

112. $m \div 6 = 9$

113. $x + 10 = 20$

114. $x \times 9 = 81$

Name:_______________ Date: ____________

115. $7 + y = 12$

116. $m \times 6 = 30$

117. $3 + 5x = 13$

118. $y \div 2 = 2$

119. $30 \div m = 5$

120. $4m + 10 = 46$

121. $4 + k = 11$

122. $k + 1 = 6$

123. $2m + 10 = 22$

124. $5 + 3k = 8$

125. $3 + 2y = 9$

126. $9 - z = 5$

Equations (Two Sides)

Solve for the variable.

127. $7k + 6 = 30 + k$

128. $4y = 9 + y$

129. $21 - x = 2x$

130. $5x = 20 + x$

131. $6 + 2y = 9 - y$

132. $6k + 8 = 64 - k$

133. $5 + m = 2m$

134. $49 + z = 7 + 7z$

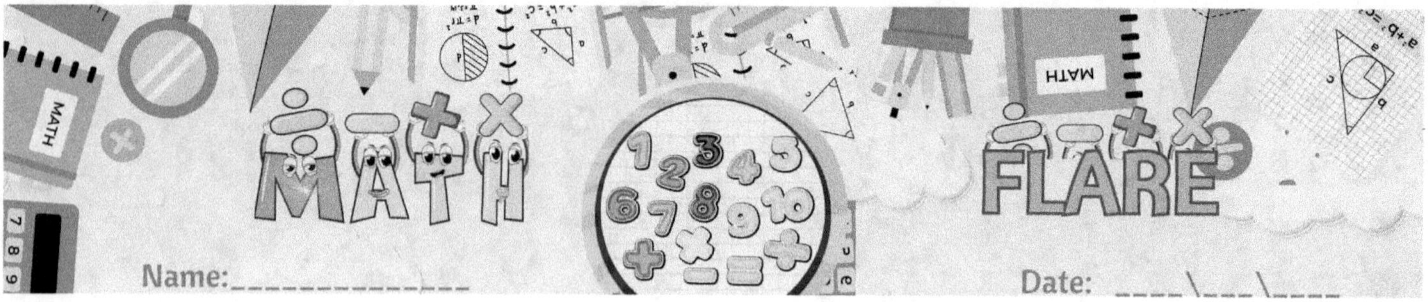

Name:______________ Date: ____________

135. $8y = 18 - y$

136. $24 + z = 5z$

137. $49 - x = 4 + 4x$

138. $4 + 3m = 20 + m$

139. $8 + 5y = 62 - y$

140. $48 - m = 7m$

141. $3m = 4 + m$

142. $28 + x = 6x + 8$

143. $9 + 2k = 18 + k$

144. $4x + 5 = 20 + x$

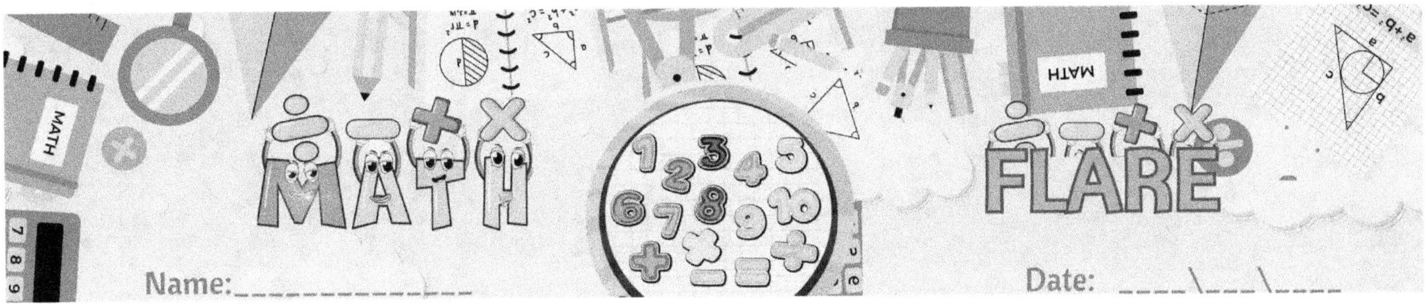

145. $14 + k = 5 + 4k$

146. $5 + 2y = 11 - y$

147. $23 + k = 3 + 6k$

148. $16 + z = 3z$

149. $2m + 4 = 8 + m$

150. $2m = 15 - m$

151. $25 + m = 6m$

152. $24 - z = 5z$

153. $2x + 5 = 13 + x$

154. $8m + 6 = 69 + m$

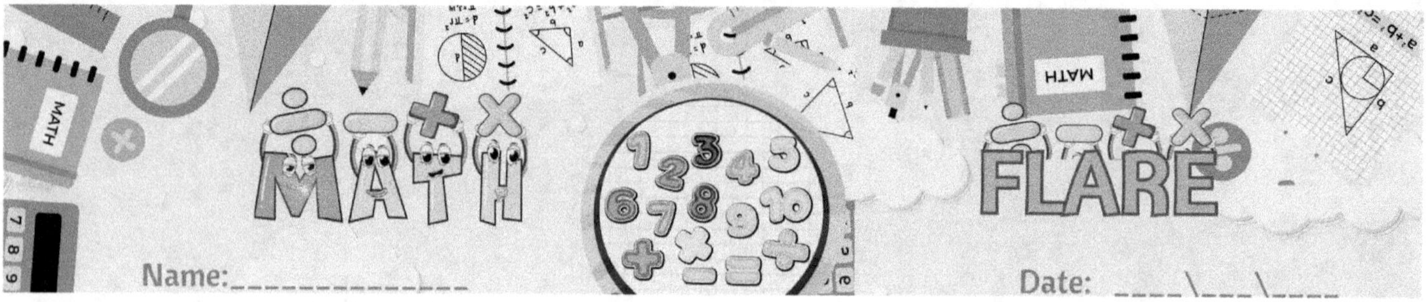

155. $36 - k = 8k$

156. $7 + 8k = 79 - k$

157. $5k = 24 + k$

158. $24 - y = 7y$

159. $8 + 4m = 38 - m$

160. $56 - x = 7x$

161. $3y + 5 = 33 - y$

162. $6z + 3 = 59 - z$

163. $47 - m = 4m + 2$

164. $5y = 20 + y$

Name:______________ Date: ____________

165. $5z = 12 + z$

166. $18 + m = 6m + 3$

167. $8x + 2 = 29 - x$

168. $11 + z = 7z + 5$

169. $6x = 28 - x$

170. $2y = 6 - y$

171. $7 + 2m = 11 + m$

172. $15 - k = 9 + 5k$

173. $3 + 2y = 5 + y$

174. $8 + 3z = 18 + z$

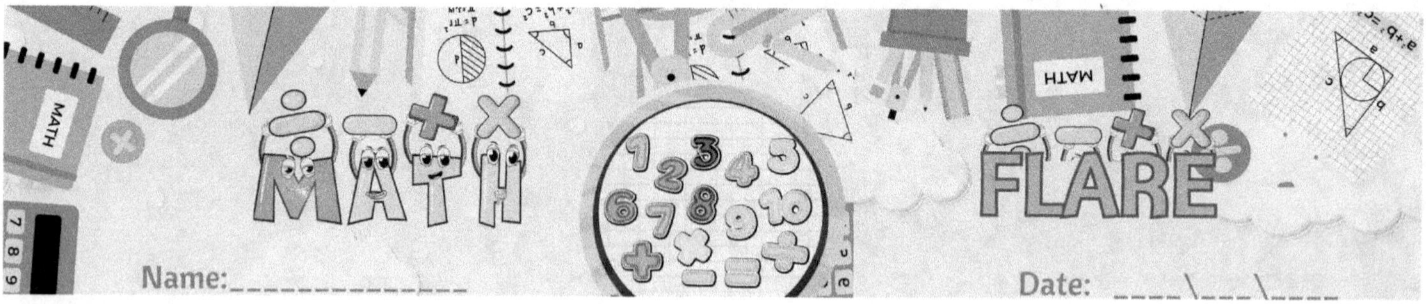

175. $17 + z = 2z + 9$

176. $12 + z = 4z + 6$

177. $7 + 2m = 10 - m$

178. $24 + k = 5k$

179. $7x + 1 = 57 - x$

180. $5 + m = 2m$

181. $6y = 21 - y$

182. $5 + 6k = 50 + k$

183. $49 + x = 8x$

184. $2k = 3 - k$

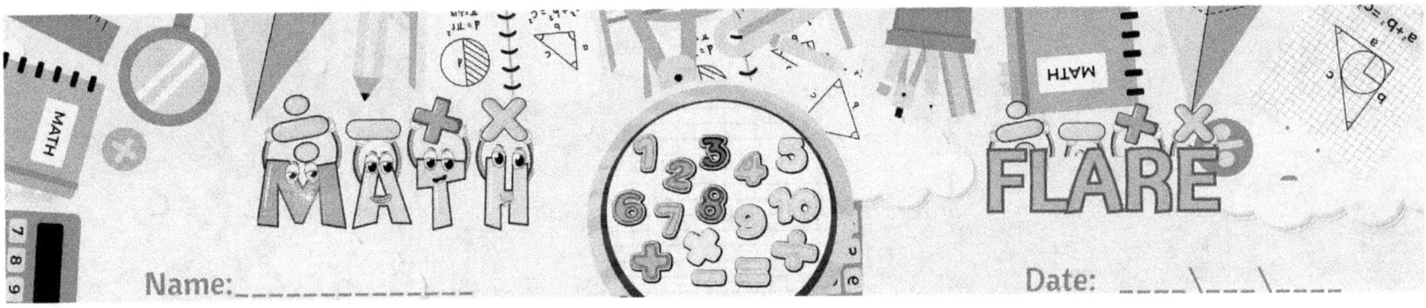

185. $16 + k = 2k + 7$

186. $1 + 2z = 25 - z$

187. $3x = 36 - x$

188. $2z = 18 - z$

189. $3y = 20 - y$

190. $5x + 9 = 21 - x$

191. $8z + 4 = 53 + z$

192. $9 + 8z = 58 + z$

193. $4z + 4 = 7 + z$

194. $2m = 18 - m$

Solving Equations

Evaluate each expression when: $x = 1$

195. $7 - x =$

196. $6x + 6x + 3x =$

197. $x + 1 + 9x =$

198. $1 + x =$

199. $9x + 4 =$

200. $6x + 10x - 2 =$

201. $6x - x =$

202. $2x - 9 =$

203. $2 + x =$

204. $5 - x =$

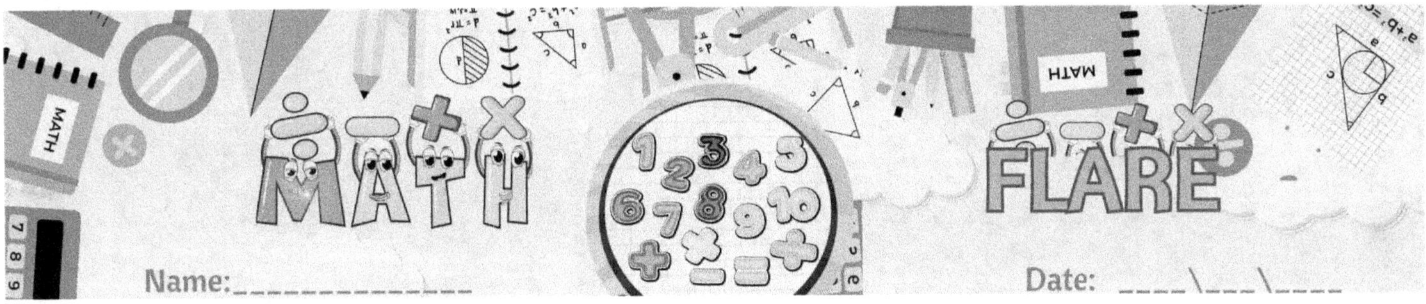

Solving Equations

Evaluate each expression when: $x = 3$

205. $10x + 4x + x =$

206. $8x + 2 - 4x =$

207. $x + 6 + 6x =$

208. $x + 1 - 7x =$

209. $10x - x =$

210. $6x + 1 - 9x =$

211. $6x + 3 - 2x =$

212. $6x + x =$

213. $4x - x =$

214. $5x + 6 =$

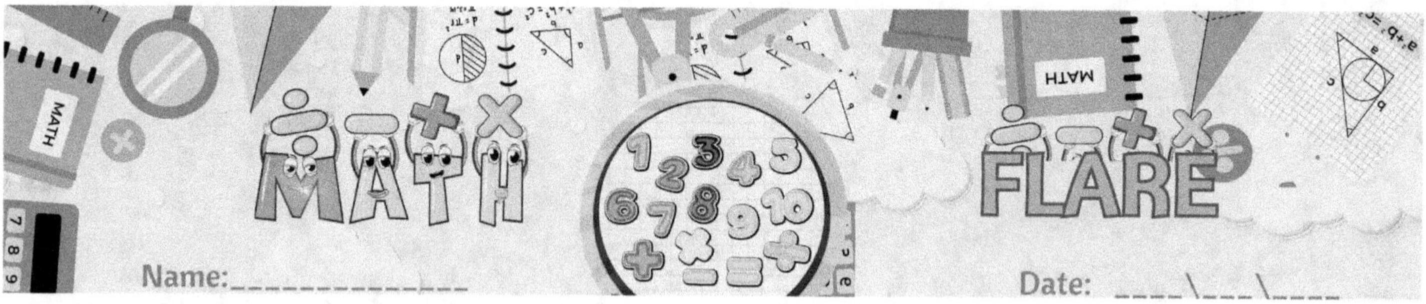

Solving Equations

Evaluate each expression when: $x = 7$

215. $6x + 5x + 2x =$

216. $9 + x =$

217. $x - 4 =$

218. $5 - x =$

219. $8x + 3 =$

220. $x + 6 + 6x =$

221. $5 + 7x =$

222. $7(5 - x) =$

223. $6(7 - x) =$

224. $2(5 - x) =$

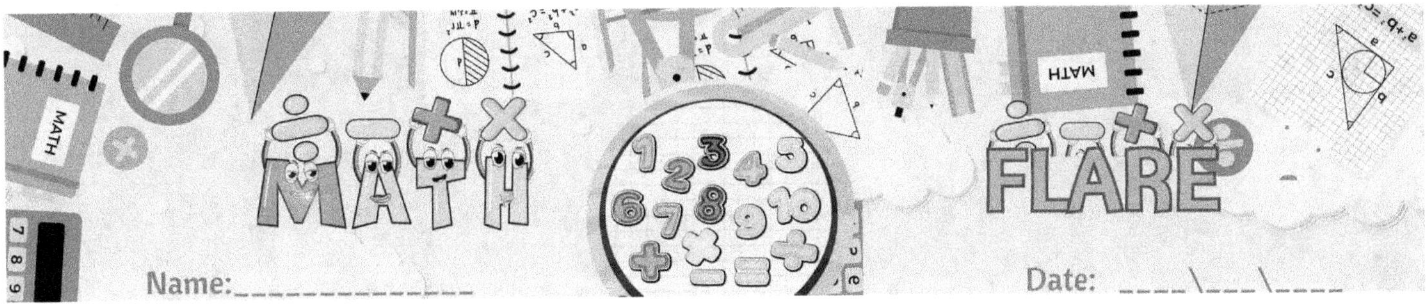

Solving Equations

Evaluate each expression when: $x = 5$

225. $x - 8 =$

226. $x + 5 + 9x =$

227. $8x + x + x =$

228. $7x + 8 =$

229. $x - 7 =$

230. $9 + x =$

231. $x + 7 + 9x =$

232. $x + 2 =$

233. $x - 9 =$

234. $10 + x =$

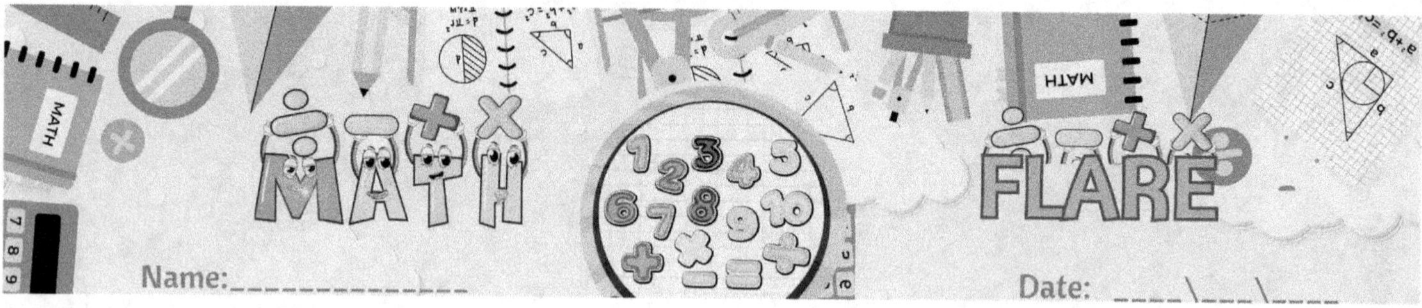

Solving Equations

Evaluate each expression when: $x = 2$

235. $8(1 + x) =$

236. $x - 2 =$

237. $3x + 10x + 4x =$

238. $4x + 6 - 9x =$

239. $x - 1 =$

240. $7x + 10 - 7x =$

241. $5x + 10 - 10x =$

242. $6 + 6x =$

243. $1 + 5x =$

244. $x + 5 + 10x =$

Solving Equations

Evaluate each expression when: $x = 1$

245. $x - 8 =$

246. $3 + 6x =$

247. $6(4 + x) =$

248. $9x + 4x - 5 =$

249. $x + 6 =$

250. $x + 1 =$

251. $9x + 4x - 9 =$

252. $x - 1 =$

253. $3x + 4x + 4x =$

254. $2x + 6x + 5x =$

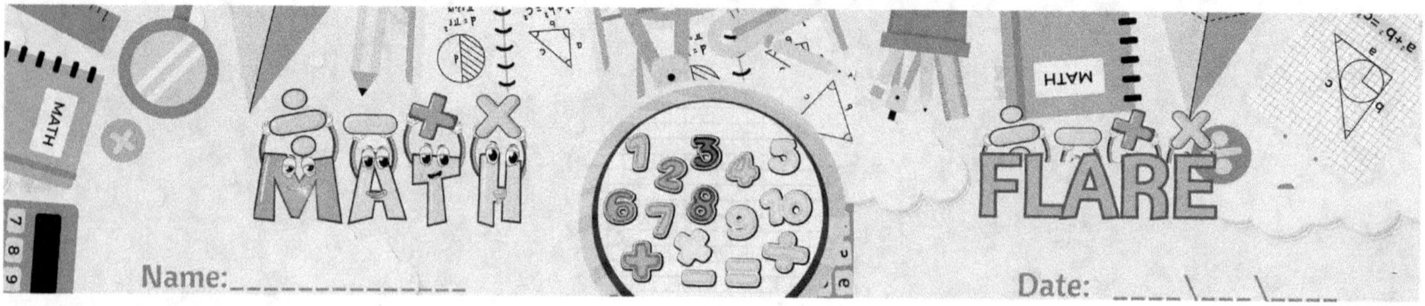

Solving Equations

Evaluate each expression when: $x = 6$

255. $8x + x =$

256. $3 + x =$

257. $10x + x =$

258. $2x + 5x + 4x =$

259. $2x + 6 =$

260. $x + 7 =$

261. $x + 10 - 10x =$

262. $x - 6 =$

263. $x - 9 =$

264. $x + 1 + 7x =$

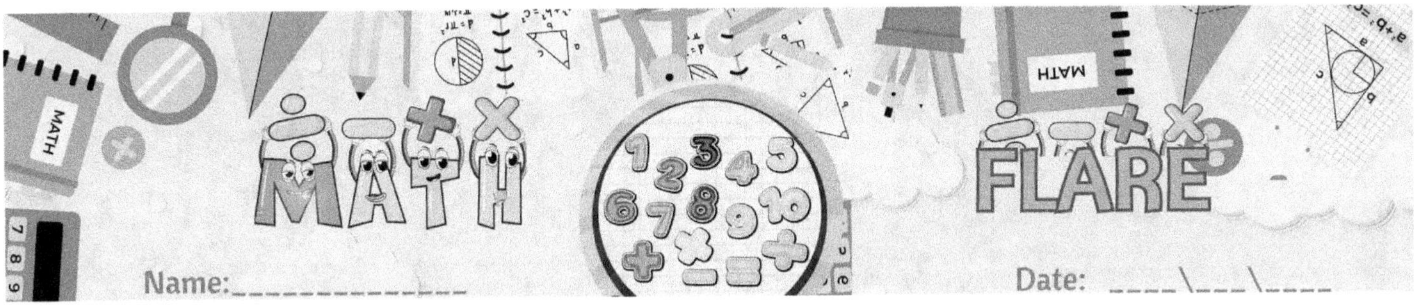

Solving Equations

Evaluate each expression when: $x = 5$

265. $10x + 6 =$

266. $3x + 1 =$

267. $3x + 2 =$

268. $2(1 + x) =$

269. $1 - x =$

270. $x - x =$

271. $x + 9 =$

272. $9x + 9 =$

273. $x + 10 =$

274. $8x + 1 =$

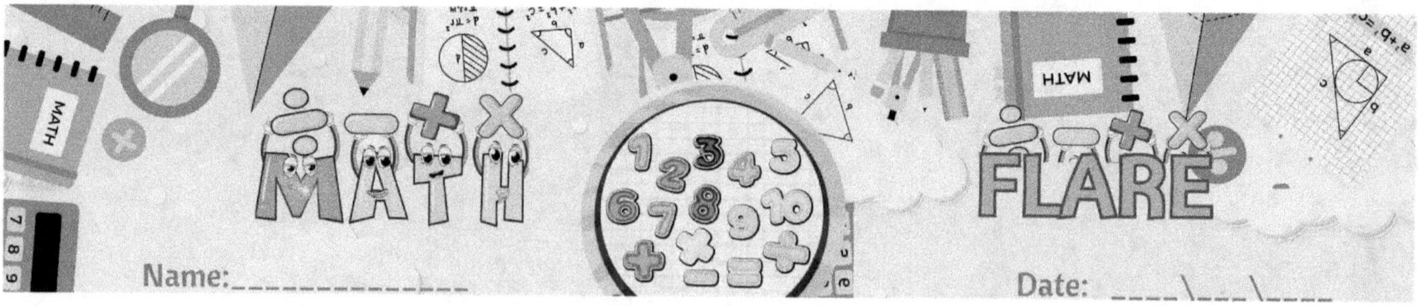

Name:_______________ Date: ____________

Solving Equations

Evaluate each expression when: $x = 7$

275. $4x - 9 =$

276. $10x + 8 =$

277. $7(8 + x) =$

278. $3x + x =$

279. $x + 1 + 4x =$

280. $x + 7x + 8x =$

281. $4x + 8 =$

282. $1 + x =$

283. $6x + 10x + 8x =$

284. $10(10 - x) =$

Solving Equations

Evaluate each expression when: $x = 2$

285. $10x + x =$

286. $3x + 2 =$

287. $7x + x =$

288. $2 + x =$

289. $3 + x =$

290. $3x + 3 =$

291. $8x - 9 =$

292. $5x + x + 2x =$

293. $9x + x =$

294. $x - 4 =$

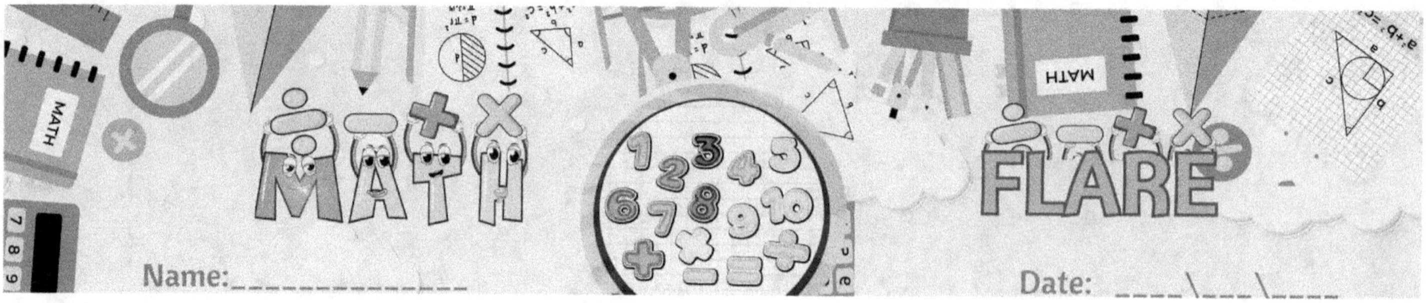

Solving Equations

Evaluate each expression when: $x = 3$

295. $x + 3 =$

296. $6 + 3x =$

297. $10x + 7 =$

298. $8 + x =$

299. $x + 6 =$

300. $3x + 2 =$

301. $9x - 5 =$

302. $x + 7 + 5x =$

303. $7x + 3 =$

304. $1 + 7x =$

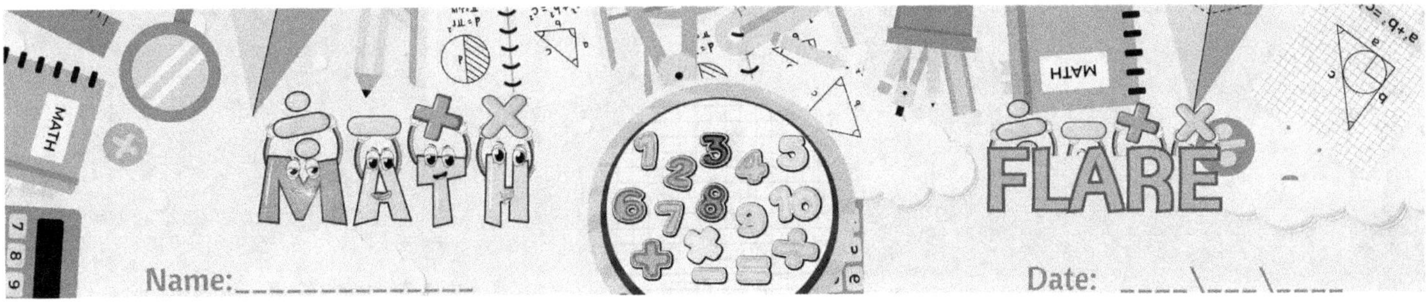

Solving Equations

Evaluate each expression when: $x = 2$

305. $x + 4 =$

306. $3x + 3 =$

307. $9(2 + x) =$

308. $10x + 3 =$

309. $6x - 5 =$

310. $4x - 5 =$

311. $x - 8 =$

312. $6x + 3 =$

313. $4(7 - x) =$

314. $3(6 - x) =$

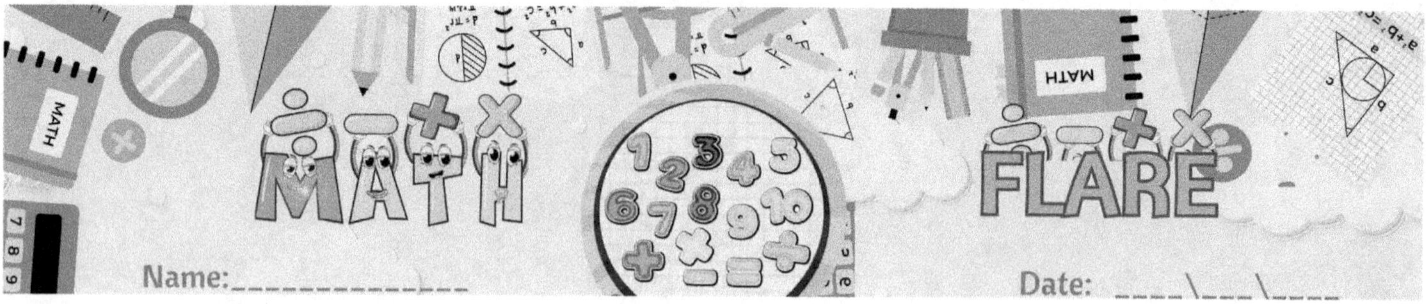

Solving Equations

Evaluate each expression when: $x = 4$

315. $x + 5 + 6x =$

316. $x + 2 =$

317. $3x + 3 =$

318. $7x + 6 =$

319. $3x - x =$

320. $9x + x =$

321. $3x + 8 =$

322. $x + 4 =$

323. $5x - x =$

324. $6 + x =$

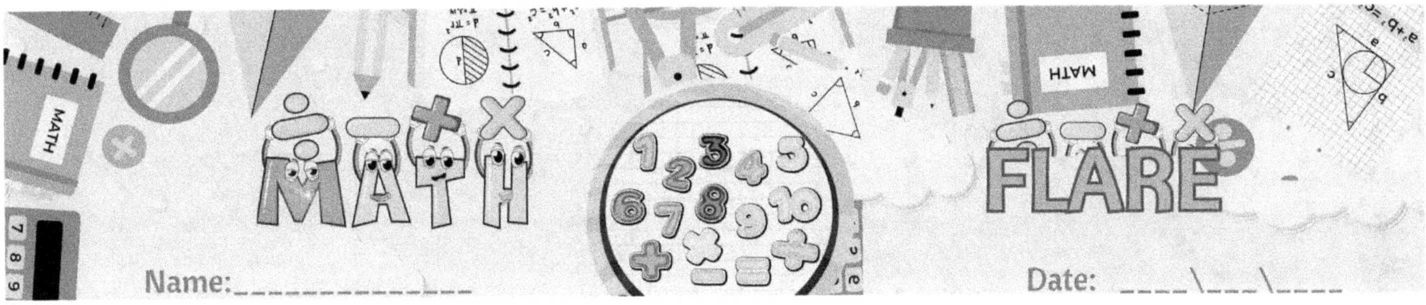

Solving Equations

Evaluate each expression when: $x = 6$

325. $1 + 4x =$

326. $7(10 - x) =$

327. $8x - x =$

328. $2 - x =$

329. $9 - x =$

330. $9x + 4 =$

331. $x + 5 + 4x =$

332. $5x + 7 =$

333. $5(4 + x) =$

334. $4x + 8 =$

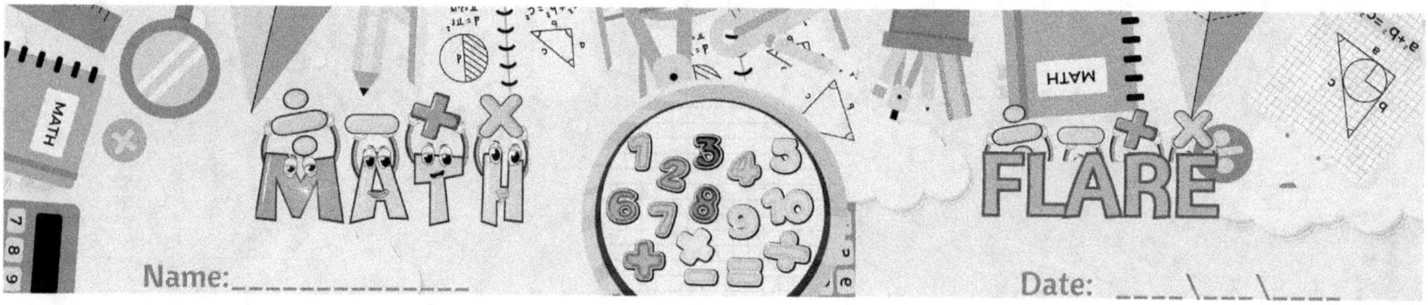

Solving Equations

Evaluate each expression when: $x = 3$

335. $9x + 2x + 7x =$

336. $3x + x - 6 =$

337. $x + 9 =$

338. $3x + 4x + x =$

339. $x + 4 =$

340. $x - 4 =$

341. $x - 7 =$

342. $x + 2 + x =$

343. $8x + 5 =$

344. $4 + x =$

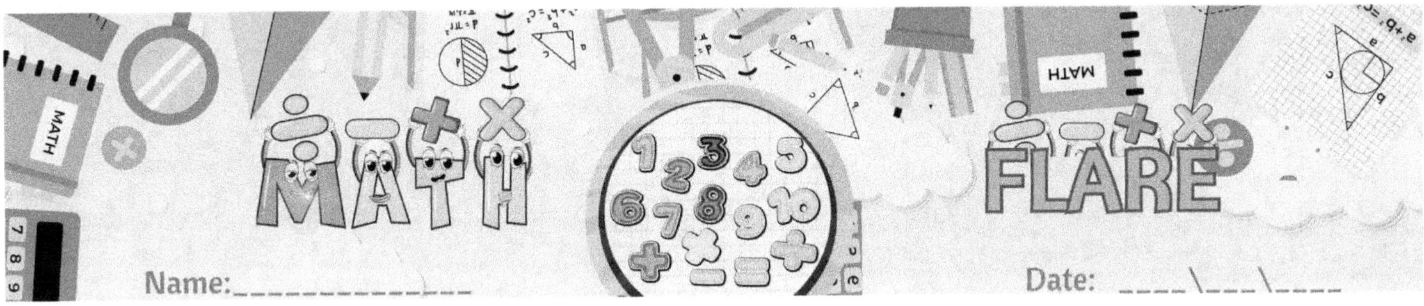

Solving Equations

Evaluate each expression when: $x = 7$

345. $5x + 3x - 8 =$

346. $6(10 - x) =$

347. $2x + 8 - 2x =$

348. $5 + 2x =$

349. $6 + x =$

350. $x + 9 + 8x =$

351. $x - 9 =$

352. $4x + x + x =$

353. $x + 2 =$

354. $8x + x =$

Solving Equations

Evaluate each expression when: $x = 2$

355. $9(5 + x) =$

356. $5 + 6x =$

357. $7x + 7x - 8 =$

358. $8 + x =$

359. $x - 10 =$

360. $3(8 - x) =$

361. $1 + x =$

362. $2 + 2x =$

363. $9x + 4 =$

364. $4x + 1 =$

Name:_______________ Date: ____________

Solving Inequalities

365. $-4 \geq -8m$

366. $8 < \dfrac{m}{2}$

367. $z - 7 < 8$

368. $-1 < 1 + x$

Name:________________ Date: _____________

369. $\frac{x}{3} < -5$

370. $k - -1 \leq 8$

371. $-5 < 5z$

372. $8 + z < -10$

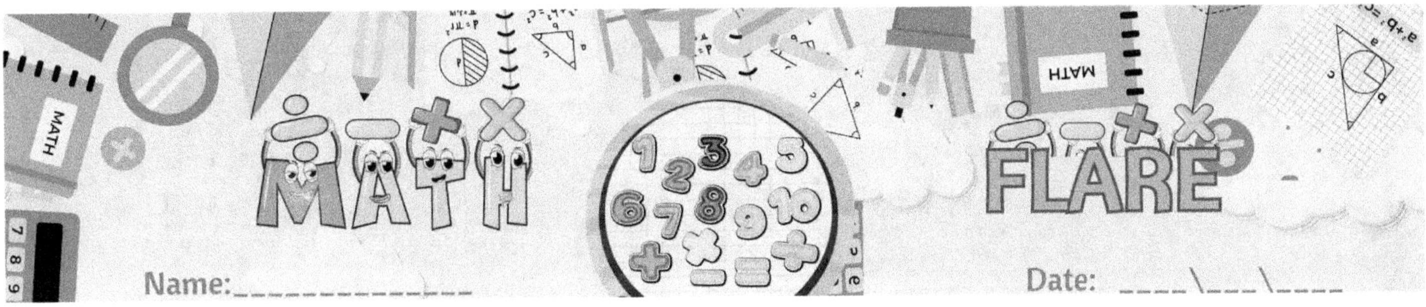

Name:______________ Date: ___________

373. $4 \leq m - -8$

374. $-4 \geq \frac{x}{6}$

375. $-2 + k < -4$

376. $4 > -8m$

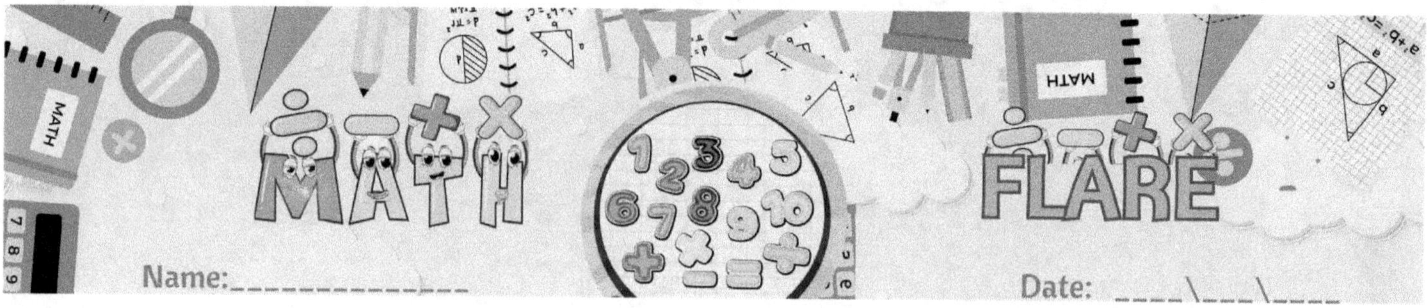

377. $\frac{z}{3} > -5$

378. $-4 > -6x$

379. $m + 1 < -9$

380. $-6 - z > -4$

Name:_______________ Date: ____________

381. $-8 \le m + -4$

382. $-6 < \frac{m}{-3}$

383. $7m \le -5$

384. $6 \ge m - 1$

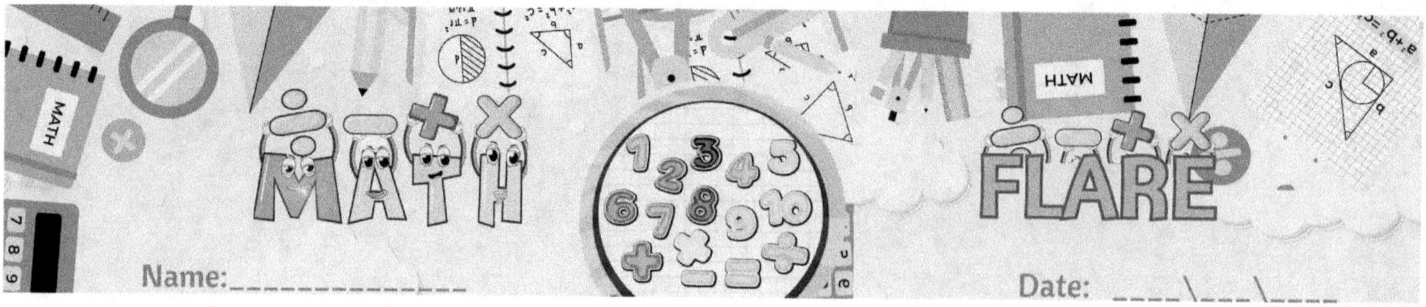

385. $m + 6 \leq -5$

386. $\frac{k}{-1} < 2$

387. $20x \geq -8$

388. $-6 - x \leq -1$

389. $2 \geq \frac{x}{-6}$

390. $-9 \leq z + 9$

391. $15x \leq -15$

392. $m - 3 \geq 9$

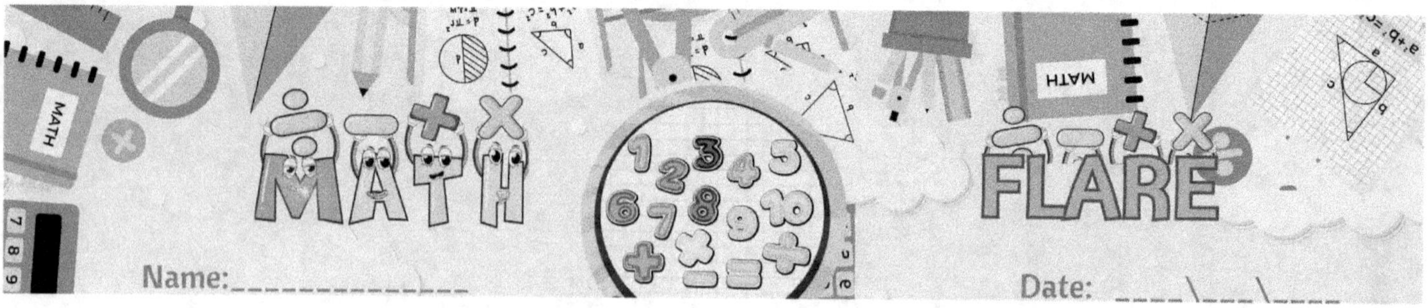

Name:_______________ Date: ____________

393. $-2 \leq \frac{z}{7}$

394. $-7 - x \leq -4$

395. $y + 3 > 3$

396. $-18x < -12$

397. $1k < -2$

398. $z + 2 \geq -5$

399. $\frac{y}{4} < -2$

400. $9 \geq 3 - x$

Name:______________ Date: ____________

401. $\frac{y}{3} \leq -1$

402. $10 < 6m$

403. $7 - k > 8$

404. $-8 + x > -1$

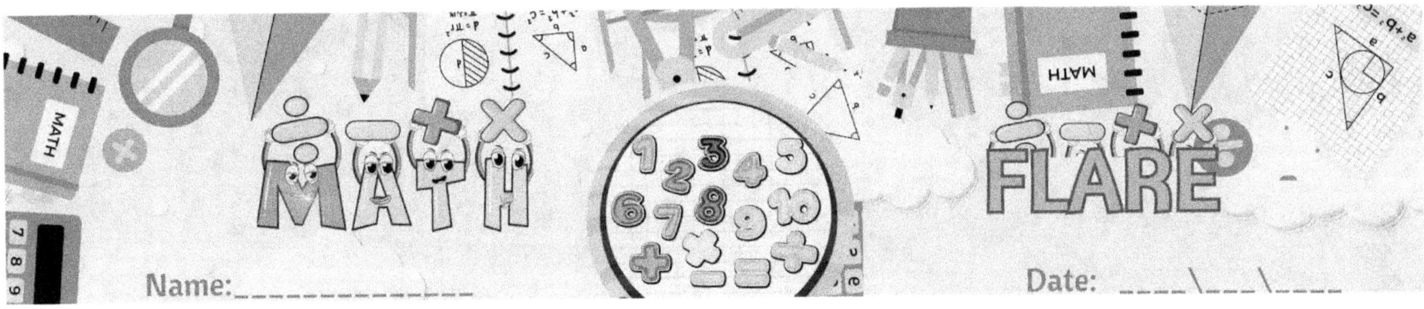

405. $-2 + m \geq 5$

406. $-2 > -3z$

407. $z - -3 \geq 1$

408. $4 > \frac{x}{2}$

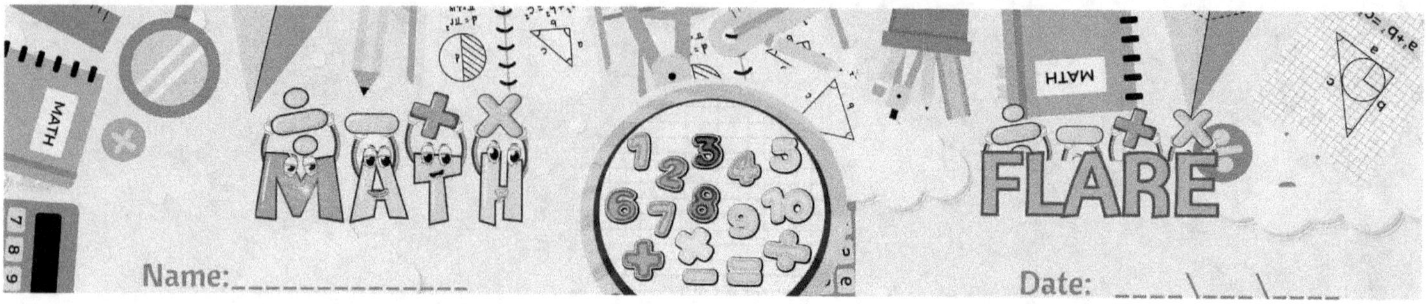

409. $-6 \leq 4m$

410. $9 < y + -7$

411. $\frac{z}{8} < -2$

412. $9 < -2 - y$

413. $6 < -12k$

414. $0 \geq -6 - x$

415. $7 > \frac{x}{-3}$

416. $-2 + y > 7$

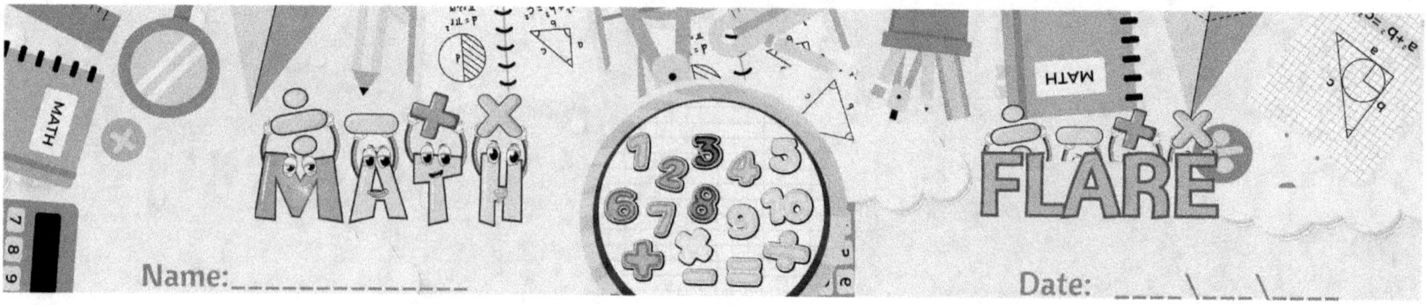

417. $\frac{z}{-6} < -3$

418. $8 + k \leq -10$

419. $-3 \leq -1z$

420. $7 > k - -6$

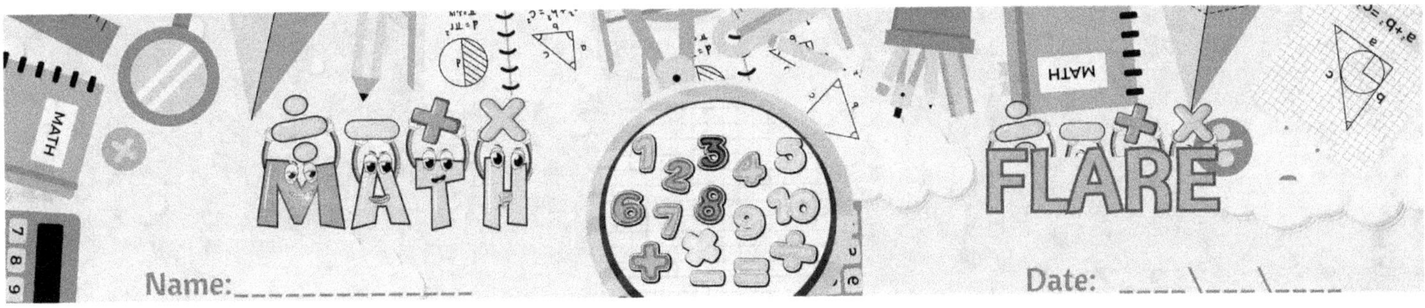

421. $9 < y - 8$

422. $10x > 6$

423. $\frac{z}{-5} < -2$

424. $4 + x \geq -6$

Name:______________ Date: ___________

425. $-20 < -16y$

426. $-9 > \frac{y}{8}$

427. $4 + z \leq -7$

428. $4 - y < 5$

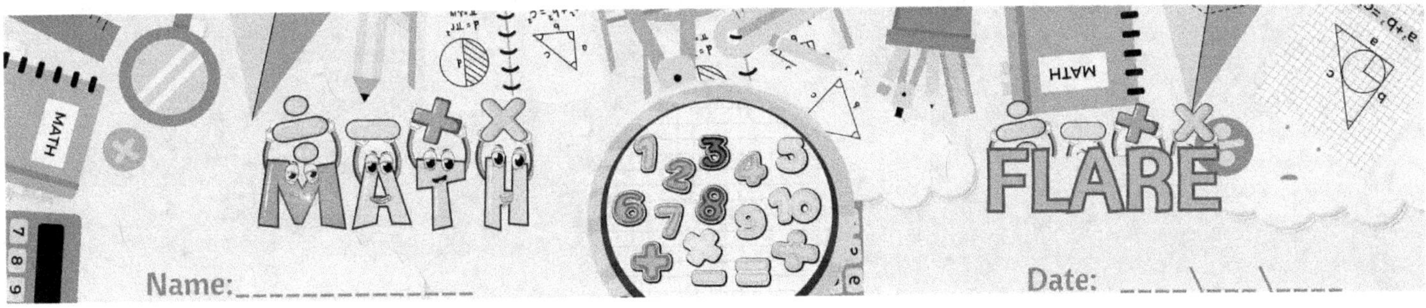

429. $-3 > -2y$

430. $8 < 3 + y$

431. $6 - k \le 9$

432. $\frac{k}{-9} < 6$

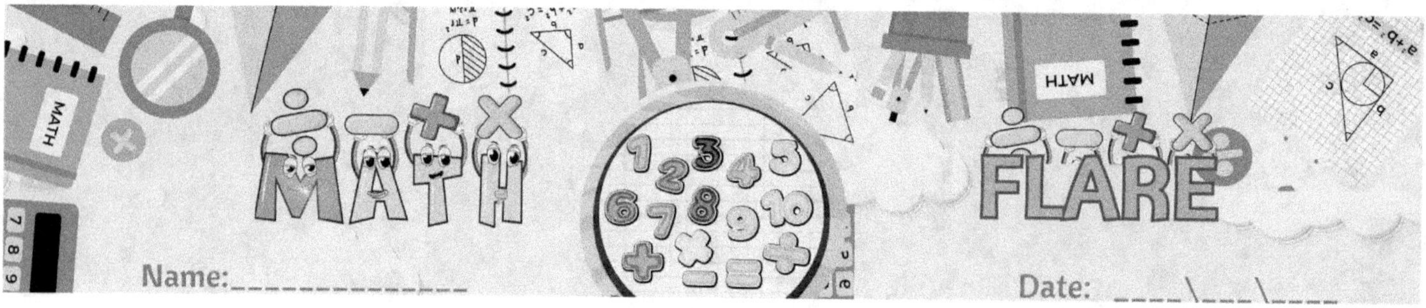

433. $-7 + y < -1$

434. $-3 < \frac{z}{7}$

435. $5 > 2 - m$

436. $-24 \leq 12k$

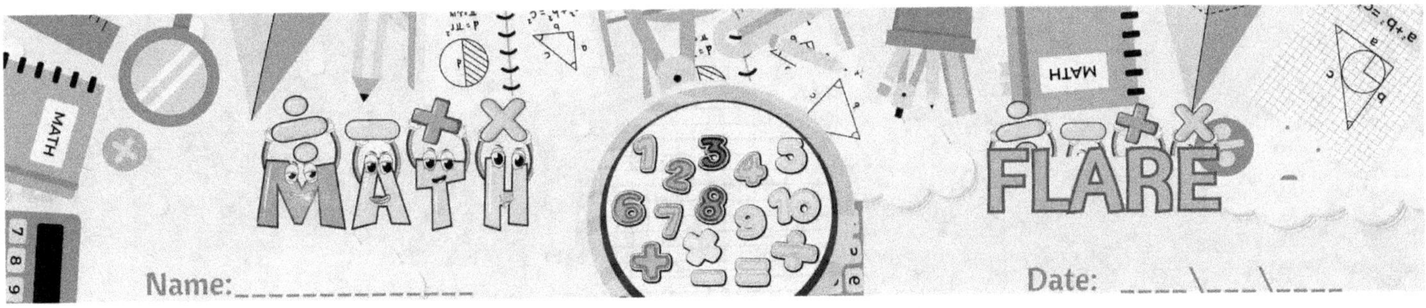

437. $-8 > \frac{m}{5}$

438. $1 + y \leq 7$

439. $3k \geq 6$

440. $9 > 7 - m$

Name:______________ Date: ____________

441. $5 < 4 - m$

442. $18 > -6k$

443. $-2 + k < 5$

444. $\frac{y}{1} < -7$

ANSWERS

Page 1: Order of Operations (PEMDAS)

1. 9	2. 73	3. 1.4	4. 22	5. 2,918	6. 37
7. 105	8. 32	9. 11	10. 81	11. 9	12. 126
13. 5	14. 198	15. 20	16. 168	17. 63	18. 18
19. 346	20. 4	21. 786	22. 105	23. 250	24. 64
25. 28	26. 137	27. 338	28. 21	29. 405	30. 3,602
31. 224	32. 103	33. 288	34. 80	35. 12	36. 270
37. 196	38. 72	39. 5	40. 44	41. 2.8	42. 46
43. 15	44. 19	45. 13	46. 72	47. 21	48. 3
49. 6	50. 18	51. 10	52. 121	53. 202	54. 64
55. 96	56. 909	57. 10	58. 1,603	59. 8,102	60. 24
61. 120	62. 904	63. 8	64. 274	65. 16	66. 7
67. 128	68. 238				

Page 8: Equations (One Side)

69. $k = 8$	70. $z = 2$	71. $y = 10$	72. $y = 48$	73. $k = 1$
74. $k = 6$	75. $k = 2$	76. $y = 5$	77. $k = 7$	78. $k = 7$
79. $k = 8$	80. $y = 5$	81. $z = 4$	82. $k = 7$	83. $k = 40$
84. $z = 1$	85. $x = 4$	86. $y = 15$	87. $z = 18$	88. $m = 2$
89. $z = 2$	90. $k = 9$	91. $m = 3$	92. $z = 4$	93. $m = 10$
94. $x = 8$	95. $z = 6$	96. $y = 1$	97. $y = 2$	98. $k = 3$

99. $z = 2$	100. $z = 6$	101. $x = 3$	102. $k = 3$	103. $m = 10$
104. $k = 9$	105. $k = 36$	106. $x = 5$	107. $z = 9$	108. $x = 4$
109. $k = 2$	110. $y = 9$	111. $k = 8$	112. $m = 54$	113. $x = 10$
114. $x = 9$	115. $y = 5$	116. $m = 5$	117. $x = 2$	118. $y = 4$
119. $m = 6$	120. $m = 9$	121. $k = 7$	122. $k = 5$	123. $m = 6$
124. $k = 1$	125. $y = 3$	126. $z = 4$		

Page 13: Equations (Two Sides)

127. $k = 4$	128. $y = 3$	129. $x = 7$	130. $x = 5$	131. $y = 1$
132. $k = 8$	133. $m = 5$	134. $z = 7$	135. $y = 2$	136. $z = 6$
137. $x = 9$	138. $m = 8$	139. $y = 9$	140. $m = 6$	141. $m = 2$
142. $x = 4$	143. $k = 9$	144. $x = 5$	145. $k = 3$	146. $y = 2$
147. $k = 4$	148. $z = 8$	149. $m = 4$	150. $m = 5$	151. $m = 5$
152. $z = 4$	153. $x = 8$	154. $m = 9$	155. $k = 4$	156. $k = 8$
157. $k = 6$	158. $y = 3$	159. $m = 6$	160. $x = 7$	161. $y = 7$
162. $z = 8$	163. $m = 9$	164. $y = 5$	165. $z = 3$	166. $m = 3$
167. $x = 3$	168. $z = 1$	169. $x = 4$	170. $y = 2$	171. $m = 4$
172. $k = 1$	173. $y = 2$	174. $z = 5$	175. $z = 8$	176. $z = 2$
177. $m = 1$	178. $k = 6$	179. $x = 7$	180. $m = 5$	181. $y = 3$
182. $k = 9$	183. $x = 7$	184. $k = 1$	185. $k = 9$	186. $z = 8$
187. $x = 9$	188. $z = 6$	189. $y = 5$	190. $x = 2$	191. $z = 7$
192. $z = 7$	193. $z = 1$	194. $m = 6$		

Page 20: Solving Equations

195. 6 196. 15 197. 11 198. 2 199. 13 200. 14 201. 5 202. -7

203. 3 204. 4

Page 21: Solving Equations

205. 45 206. 14 207. 27 208. -17 209. 27 210. -8 211. 15

212. 21 213. 9 214. 21

Page 22: Solving Equations

215. 91 216. 16 217. 3 218. -2 219. 59 220. 55 221. 54

222. -14 223. 0 224. -4

Page 23: Solving Equations

225. -3 226. 55 227. 50 228. 43 229. -2 230. 14 231. 57

232. 7 233. -4 234. 15

Page 24: Solving Equations

235. 24 236. 0 237. 34 238. -4 239. 1 240. 10 241. 0

242. 18 243. 11 244. 27

Page 25: Solving Equations

245. -7 246. 9 247. 30 248. 8 249. 7 250. 2 251. 4

252. 0 253. 11 254. 13

Page 26: Solving Equations

255. 54 256. 9 257. 66 258. 66 259. 18 260. 13 261. -44

262. 0 263. -3 264. 49

Page 27: Solving Equations

265. 56 266. 16 267. 17 268. 12 269. -4 270. 0 271. 14

272. 54 273. 15 274. 41

Page 28: Solving Equations

275. 19 276. 78 277. 105 278. 28 279. 36 280. 112 281. 36

282. 8 283. 168 284. 30

Page 29: Solving Equations

285. 22 286. 8 287. 16 288. 4 289. 5 290. 9 291. 7

292. 16 293. 20 294. -2

Page 30: Solving Equations

295. 6 296. 15 297. 37 298. 11 299. 9 300. 11 301. 22

302. 25 303. 24 304. 22

Page 31: Solving Equations

305. 6 306. 9 307. 36 308. 23 309. 7 310. 3 311. -6

312. 15 313. 20 314. 12

Page 32: Solving Equations

315. 33 316. 6 317. 15 318. 34 319. 8 320. 40 321. 20

322. 8 323. 16 324. 10

Page 33: Solving Equations

325. 25 326. 28 327. 42 328. -4 329. 3 330. 58 331. 35

332. 37 333. 50 334. 32

Page 34: Solving Equations

335. 54   336. 6   337. 12   338. 24   339. 7   340. -1   341. -4

342. 8   343. 29   344. 7

Page 35: Solving Equations

345. 48   346. 18   347. 8   348. 19   349. 13   350. 72   351. -2

352. 42   353. 9   354. 63

Page 36: Solving Equations

355. 63   356. 17   357. 20   358. 10   359. -8   360. 18   361. 3

362. 6   363. 22   364. 9

Page 37: Solving Inequalities

365. $m \geq 1/2$ 366. $m > 16$ 367. $z < 15$ 368. $x > -2$

369. $x < -15$ 370. $k \leq 7$ 371. $z > -1$ 372. $z < -18$

373. $m \geq -4$ 374. $x \leq -24$ 375. $k < -2$ 376. $m > -1/2$

377. $z > -15$ 378. $x > 2/3$ 379. $m < -10$ 380. $z < -2$

381. $m \geq -4$ 382. $m < 18$ 383. $m \leq -5/7$ 384. $m \leq 7$

385. $m \leq -11$ 386. $k > -2$ 387. $x \geq -2/5$ 388. $x \geq -5$

389. $x \geq -12$ 390. $z \geq -18$ 391. $x \leq -1$ 392. $m \geq 12$

393. $z \geq -14$ 394. $x \geq -3$ 395. $y > 0$ 396. $x > 2/3$

397. $k < -2$ 398. $z \geq -7$ 399. $y < -8$ 400. $x \geq -6$

401. $y \leq -3$ 402. $m > 5/3$ 403. $k < -1$ 404. $x > 7$

405. $m \geq 7$ 406. $z > 2/3$ 407. $z \geq -2$ 408. $x < 8$

409. $m \geq -3/2$ 410. $y > 16$ 411. $z < -16$ 412. $y < -11$

413. $k < -1/2$	414. $x \geq -6$	415. $x > -21$	416. $y > 9$
417. $z > 18$	418. $k \leq -18$	419. $z \leq 3$	420. $k < 1$
421. $y > 17$	422. $x > 3/5$	423. $z > 10$	424. $x \geq -10$
425. $y < 5/4$	426. $y < -72$	427. $z \leq -11$	428. $y > -1$
429. $y > 3/2$	430. $y > 5$	431. $k \geq -3$	432. $k > -54$
433. $y < 6$	434. $z > -21$	435. $m > -3$	436. $k \geq -2$
437. $m < -40$	438. $y \leq 6$	439. $k \geq 2$	440. $m > -2$
441. $m < -1$	442. $k > -3$	443. $k < 7$	444. $y < -7$

www.ingramcontent.com/pod-product-compliance
Lightning Source LLC
LaVergne TN
LVHW060620090726
842905LV00038B/756
* 9 7 9 8 8 6 9 3 7 5 0 2 5 *